Retire Now

Retire Now

simple solutions for retirement

MICHAEL A. STERANKA

Co-Author of *The E Myth Financial Advisor*

MikeSteranka.com
8530 Veterans Highway, 2nd Floor
Millersville, MD 21108
443.308.5216

First Edition

ISBN: 978-1-939758-02-6 (paperback)
ISBN: 978-1-939758-01-9 (ebook)

Printed in the United States of America on acid-free paper.

Book Design by Dotti Albertine

SPECIAL DISCLAIMER
The contents of this book are meant to be informational only. You should consult your legal, tax and financial advisor before implementing any ideas suggested herein.

Mr. Steranka is held harmless for any actions or inactions individuals may take or not take because of the information in this book. Mr. Steranka is not acting as a fiduciary in his capacity as author of this work.

Five Star Marketing and Consulting, LLC, also waves any liability for publishing this work.

I would like to dedicate this book to the thousands of retirees I have met over the last twenty years who have shared their lives and their families with me. They have encouraged me to learn more about them and their needs and concerns. Any success I have enjoyed is due to the sharing that these folks have had with me and my firm. We truly appreciate helping any retiree improve their retirement outlook.

CONTENTS

9   *Introduction*

11   Chapter One **It's Time to Give Yourself a Pension**

23   Chapter Two **The House Always Wins**

29   Chapter Three **The Rise of the "DIY Pension Plan"**

41   Chapter Four **Leaving A Financial Legacy**

53   Chapter Five **Leveraging Your Life Insurance**

65   Chapter Six **What About Your Health?**

77   Chapter Seven **What About the Future?**

87   Chapter Eight **Should We Talk?**

91   *About the Author*

93   *Special Note from Mike Steranka*

INTRODUCTION

Some people like roller coasters. They like the thrill of high-speed ups and downs. They like that nervous feeling in the pit of their stomachs when the roller coaster seemingly spins out of control. They even like the heart stopping sensation of being upside down, if only for a few terrifying moments.

Those high-speed ups and downs are terrific at the theme park. But they have no place in your retirement strategy!

If your hard-earned savings are riding a roller coaster that seems to have more downs than ups, or bigger downs than ups, then you will definitely benefit from the ideas in this short book. The basic idea is this: there's nothing that provides the safety and security of a pension. And since most employers won't give you a pension these days, or are in danger of defaulting on their pension commitments, the best way to get a pension...is to give it to yourself.

You don't have to worry about whether you'll outlive your money. Not if you invest it in such a way that you have guaranteed income coming to you month after month, for the rest of your life, and also the security of knowing that your loved ones will be well taken care of after you're gone.

If the idea of giving yourself a pension sounds appealing, take a little time and consider the ideas I'm about to share with you.

Take your grandkids on the rollercoaster. But not your savings.

— **Mike Steranka**
August, 2011

Chapter One

It's Time to Give Yourself a Pension

In the good old days you worked for the same company for some 30 or 40 years. At the end of that term, you retired. The company sometimes threw a retirement party for you, maybe gave you a gold watch, and then sent you on your way. Life was good.

In return for your years of loyal service, you would get a pension check in your mailbox every month for the rest of your life. That was guaranteed, stable income for the remainder of your years. Just twenty-five years ago, two thirds of retirement community relied on pension plans. But when we think of pensions today, we think of grandpa and the gold watch. That's not too sexy.

Today, twice as many people have 401(k) plans as they do pension plans. Outside of the public sector, we've seen a dramatic reduction, even elimination, of the use of pension plans for retirement benefits. 401(k) plans have become popular because you can make your own investment decisions, have a balanced portfolio with more options, more accessibility, and more freedom to do as you wish with your retirement savings.

Sound great?

Here's the catch: people are now discovering that they aren't saving enough nor are they investing wisely. They are looking hard at their savings and going, "You know something? I'm not going to make it on this." More and more, people are realizing that their savings only provide a small percentage of their paycheck and their investments are not going to last for as long as they live.

Since the economic collapse of 2008, people are also discovering that their 401(k)s are now, as the not-so-funny joke goes, just 201(k) s. Smart, savvy people are realizing that their savings and investments aren't growing at a sustainable rate. When people try and earn $40,000 or $50,000 each year off a million dollar investment in the markets, just so they can afford their standard of living, they need to ask themselves if the markets go up every single year.

The answer is no.

Sure, sometime the markets are up a lot one year, but there are also other years when they are down even more. This has very much been the case recently. So, it really depends on when you retire. Is your investment strategy centered on hoping that the market gets lucky for five to ten years before the market falls off a cliff? And are you willing to risk having your investments fall off that same cliff during your retirement?

Smart people realize what's at stake and that's the reason why there are trillions of dollars in money market accounts today. People are more willing to lose one to two percent to inflation by keeping their savings in cash than risking their net worth drop by 40% or 50% or more, as it did in 2008.

So then people think: "Wouldn't it be great if my company or my job could give me a pension just the way grandpa got one?" And that's the problem — companies now won't.

When the use of pension plans decreased, the burden of responsibility for providing income for the lifetime of an employee shifted from the company to the employee. In addition, the burden of risk also shifted and companies now expect you to take ownership of your retirement savings and investments to last for the rest of your life.

Moreover, you're probably not going to stay with one employer for your entire career anymore. You may well have seven different careers during the course of your lifetime, let alone seven different jobs. As a result, the only person you can rely on to give you a pension today is...*you*.

Nearly twenty years ago, I focused my financial services practice primarily on retirees. Over the course of my career, I've seen some people handle their assets very wisely and some handled them very poorly. I've met with hundreds of retirees every single year. These interactions instilled in me a sense of what is important to the retirement community. The people who don't have pensions must accumulate retirement savings. And that's not easy.

Let's say you accumulate $1 million. This may seem like a lot of money at first glance. But if you look at how that $1 million is going to pay you $40,000 or more each year for the rest of your life, and then factor in your life expectancy, your spouse's life expectancy, and potential inflation, it doesn't seem like that much anymore. Having a million dollars means little if it's not going to last you through your retirement.

The reality is that if a person is going to retire and stop generating income, even *several* million in savings may not be enough. It all depends on your lifestyle. When someone has a pension of $80,000 a year coming in from the government with a cost of living adjustment, that's equivalent to a private sector employee having around $2 million in savings. Now how many of us have $2 to $3 million saved in our retirement plan?

Not too many!

The amount of money we have socked away is less important than the sense of security that comes from having a steady flow of income. Having $150,000 a year in guaranteed income may well feel like having $10 million in the bank, because you know you will have all the money you'll need for the rest of your life.

But when you don't have that income need satisfied, you'll still worry about running out of money no matter how big your account balance. And having a higher balance won't mean anything if the principal is constantly at risk. Just because it is here today, does not mean it will be here tomorrow.

People want to feel confident that they can always stay in their home, pay their bills, have money to buy the prescription drugs they need, have enough to send their grandkids to college, or even put a down payment on a house for their kids. When they feel they continually have the resources to meet all of their needs, wants, and desires, that is when they really feel wealthy.

In this book, I want to show you how to do just that. I want to show you how to give yourself the pension that grandpa retired on. I'll show you how to create real financial security in era of financial, political, and social *insecurity*.

In my experience, the biggest concern that people often have is running out of money during their retirement. Unfortunately, this happens quite often. Nine out of every ten people ages 65 and older receive Social Security benefits, and Social Security represents the major source of income for most of the elderly . More than a third of retirees (35 percent) receive 90 percent of their income as a monthly payment from social security.

So what does that tell you?

Most people run out of money and rely on government benefits as a security net. But that's not a solution; this problem will become substantially worse in the coming years as we have more retirees and fewer people supporting them.

People are also living longer these days. Say you have a health incident that suddenly becomes a real financial burden. It is going to draw down your savings really fast. Now say the housing and stock markets tumble, causing you lose 30% to 40% of your net worth. It's so easy for a $750,000 estate to be spent down to zero over the course of a retirement. All of a sudden, the only money you have coming in is Social Security, and then you die without any assets to pass on to your children and grandchildren. It's a truly sad thing for people who worked hard all their lives.

People really need to get their money's worth from their retirement dollar in these uncertain times. And it needs to happen immediately. As a result, I see people taking on far too much risk with their savings. I've seen people coming in with a portfolio that's 100% in stock, trying to draw an income on it. In other words, their entire life savings are at constant risk. Or they might have a health situation and there may be no survivor benefits on whatever pension they might have, meaning that if they die, their spouse will have nothing. Often times, there might also only be one spouse receiving Social Security. It's gut-wrenching to see this. Sure, there is a small probability of success for people who are exposed to huge amounts of risk, or those who will survive their health problem and thus keep the pension money flowing longer. But exposure to this much risk so late in the game has a substantially higher probability of failure.

I often say to my clients, "Risk is for other people trying to get their money to be as much as you already have."

Let's say you have a million dollars. Most people would like to have a million, right? But you already have the million. Risk, in this case, may not be for you. All you have to do from here is not lose that million and set it up to pay you the "pension" I'll show you how to create. Now picture this. Imagine we could take a million dollars and design our own pension where we would receive $50,000 a year for life without putting our principal at risk. Isn't that better than risking it all on the stock market? Sure, you might make massive gains in the stock market, but you might also fall off the cliff and completely lose that million.

I often ask my clients if they would like a sure thing, or if they would like to gamble on a "maybe." If they choose the sure thing, I know that they're leaning towards creating a pension. If they say maybe, I know they want to take a lot of risk.

I'm an advocate toward taking risk when it's warranted. But there's a right way to take on risk and there's a wrong way. Most people opt for risk the wrong way--they're betting their futures instead of protecting their hard-earned cash. That's not risk; that's usually financial suicide.

There's a tool that financial analysts use called the "Monte Carlo simulation." The simulation runs sample probabilities for different variables to predict the probability of success or failure for a given allocation based on thousands of possible outcomes. In a T Rowe Price Report, issue number 110 Winter 2011, analysts took someone who retired in January, 2000 with $500,000 of retirement savings. The portfolio consisted of 55% stocks and 45% bonds, with the assumption that the individual would withdraw $20,000 a year with a 3% cost of living adjustment for a 30 year time period. So the question they asked is this: how likely is a person with that level of risk likely to achieve the financial goal of $20,000 of income plus that 3% cost of living adjustment for the next 30 years?

They had an 89% success rate when they first started, in 2000. But after 2000-2002 bear market, the probability of success went down to 46%. It rebounded in consequent years, but after the financial crisis of 2008, the probability of success was at 6%. Just six percent! At this point, a question you might ask somebody if you are designing their retirement plan is, "How confident would you be with an approach where there is a 94% probability of failure?"

The answer almost always is, "I would be afraid of running out of money." And again, that is the main concern among everyone who retires today.

Most financial planners will tell you that the market will recover over time. But do you have enough time for that recovery to occur? And how do they know for a certainty that the market will recover? Even if it does come back from a big fall, that's going to be a serious problem for someone who is retiring today, or even five to ten years from today. The market doesn't care if you are 65 or 25. It will perform the way it wants to perform. And past performance is never indicative of the future.

So if you say to a retiree aged 65 that you've got a plan that will work out over the next 20 years, he might come back and say, "Listen, I'm 65. I might only have 20 years." Most retirees won't be interested in an approach if it takes 10 or 15 years just to get back the money that's lost if the market takes another dive. And quite frankly, who's to say it won't?

When planning, I think the more prudent approach is to protect your principal and income streams, so that you have enough money to last through your retirement. And if you do have an appetite for risk, take on that risk with the extra money you have outside of your immediate needs.

Regardless of what we have, we need to have our baseline income protection. The best way accomplish this is to design our own pension plan. That's what most people are looking for today. That's what's going to make you feel like you have enough money to spend. And that's what's going to give you the feeling of wealth.

There are a wide variety of products available today in the financial services industry that allow you to create a pension using a fixed annuity or fixed indexed annuity. You want something that comes with a guarantee against principal loss. So that leaves us with fixed annuities and fixed indexed annuities. These products are guaranteed by the full faith and credit of the issuing company and are not FDIC insured.

When I mention the word "annuity", sometimes that provokes an immediate reaction. Sometimes negative, sometimes positive. The negative reactions to annuities generally stem from someone's preconceived notions or personal experience. They remember when their Aunt Sally had an annuity and received money from it for three or four years. But then she passed away, and suddenly, the money was gone.

But this is only one type of annuity and it's not the product that I would recommend to most people. In reality, fixed indexed annuities have come a long way. The pensions you can now create today through fixed indexed annuities are substantially superior to what Aunt Sally used to have. Today's fixed indexed annuities can guarantee income for life without giving away the principal (or annuitizing) when using an income benefit rider.

That's a pretty big deal!

If I give away the principal, I relinquish access to that money. When given an option of having access to the principal balance, most people prefer to have that accessibility because you never know what might happen in life. So today, there are fixed indexed annuities that don't force you to give the principal away. These products are really gaining traction in creating personal pension plans. The plans like grandpa used to have.

In my opinion, insurance companies got it right this time. They went to the income planning professionals, familiar with insurance products, who work with retirees, like myself, and asked us what our clients really want.

So, we told them.

We told them that our clients want guaranteed income for life, the ability to have a survivor benefit, the ability to reduce inflationary impact, and most importantly, they didn't want to give up control of that principal. The insurance companies really listened and created a whole series of fantastic products.

Let's look at a practical example.

Say your social security is $20,000 a year and your spouse's social security is $10,000 a year. That brings a total income level of $30,000 a year. But say you need $60,000 to meet your expenses.

Say it's determined that you need to put away $600,000 into a fixed indexed annuity to generate the additional $30,000 a year. We'll do just that. And today, we can do it with a 100% survivor benefit. The amount of annual lifetime income is determined by the persons' attained age. Immediately, you can see the benefits of doing this.

Let's say the spouse passes away. We'll lose that $10,000 of income from Social Security, but with that fixed indexed annuity, our total income only goes down from $60,000 to $50,000. Percentage-wise, that's not too bad at all. It's much better than going down from $30,000 to $20,000. Fixed indexed annuities with survivor benefits allow for that extra bit of wiggle room.

But this is a very important concept and a critical part of what I do when planning someone's income stream for their retirement. You need to look at what happens when a spouse passes away. Hopefully, the survivor will inherit the house and the other assets, but it's critical to determine what the surviving spouse's income is going to look like. Whether that happens 5 years or 15 years from now, you must solve for those needs.

Now say you have $900,000 saved instead of the $600,000. That's $300,000 of extra money you now have. That extra money is what you can use to take on some risk if you have an appetite for it. That's taking smart risks because your needs are still being met even if the worst-case scenario happens and you lose everything.

Of course, it might be wise to designate some emergency cash of $50,000 in the bank, a CD, or a money market account. Now you have $250,000 that can be invested any way that you want. Let's say you decide to keep $125,000 in bonds and $125,000 in stocks. Whatever the $250,000 investment generates is real growth because you have a balanced portfolio with liquidity and all of your income needs are still being met.

Kiplinger's Retirement Planning Guide for 2010 recommended that people use an annuity to fill the gap between expenses and guaranteed sources of income like Social Security pensions. And if you only use $50,000 instead of the $60,000 a year we allocated, that extra $10,000 can also help offset the rise in inflation. From a planning perspective, we can mathematically balance our budget and meet our needs with nearly 100% probability of success. And that far exceeds that 6% probability of success in the markets we saw earlier.

We'll explore all of these ideas in more depth as we go forward. The big picture here is the retirement landscape has really changed since the good old days. The old pension plans that benefited grandpa no longer exist, and we really need to be savvy about how we ensure our needs are met in retirement. We went through one of the biggest boom markets in the history of the world from 1982 to 2000. Things really haven't been the same since then. Yet, people are still optimistic and believe we'll have another run like that.

Generally, bull and bear markets can be hard to figure out if the trend is going against your belief system. For someone who is retired or about to retire in the next 5 years, you really can't assume risk like that until you meet the financial needs you need in retirement. In this book, I'll show you how to design a personal pension plan that will provide you with a guaranteed income stream simply by placing anywhere from $250,000 to $2 million in fixed indexed annuities. I'll teach you how to protect your savings while generating enough revenue to cover your expenses, and even offset inflation, regardless of how the markets perform. The tools and strategies you'll learn in the coming chapters will ensure that your savings last throughout your retirement and provide you with the personal and financial wealth you desire from life.

Though pension plans from private companies may have fallen by the wayside, you can still give yourself a pension today! Stick with me; I'll show you how.

Chapter Two

The House Always Wins

Despite the recent turmoil in the markets, you still see many people investing in equities or stocks. From my experience when looking over client investment accounts, not everybody is aware of how much money they have made or lost. Granted, there's always a place for risk, which generates growth. But why would anyone be willing to take on that much risk for a potentially low return?

The answer is simple. Investors are drawn to the equity markets despite the knowledge that the odds are stacked against them. Although there are always risks involved, investors in equity markets often hold the mentality that they are the exception to the rule, that they can beat the odds.

Now I'm not saying that you should avoid investing in the equity markets. Instead, you need to be honest about the risks associated with investing in equities. In this chapter, we'll take a step back and look at the whole picture to fully understand how the system works. With this information, you can make smarter decisions about the risk you assume. As briefly mentioned in Chapter 1, you only want to risk the money you can afford to lose. Similarly, you would never want to put your entire retirement savings at risk in the markets. But if you protect the money you need throughout your retirement, and invest the rest in equities, you smartly assume risk and might even make some money!

It is important to understand how the markets function. Equity markets are, first and foremost, businesses. Like all businesses, they need to turn a profit to stay in business. Wall Street is no exception. Wall Street needs investors to generate profits through the commissions and fees on the sales of financial products and the management of funds. More investors who buy products and inject funds into the marketplace mean bigger profits. When people buy more products and invest in the market, demand increases, the influx of cash investments inflates prices, and everyone makes money. As a result, Wall Street will always market itself in a way that helps it attract more investors and sell more products.

Wall Street does this by assuring investors that their products are sound investments and that you are likely to make money. Firms are incentivized to market their products by adjusting their charts to reflect the best performance in the past.

Additionally, almost every major financial publication propagates a conventional wisdom that a balanced approach to stocks and bonds is the safest way to minimize exposure to risk. You want to "diversify" your exposure to the market across all sectors. If you simply flip through the magazine and look at the advertisements, you'll find the answers. Almost all of the advertisers and sponsors of these publications are major investment firms who sell a wide array of financial products to investors like you and me. These firms are the major sources of advertising revenue for almost all of these publications that offer up investment advice.

For these reasons, it is important to be cautious and wary with the advice you receive. When it comes to investments, people have a natural tendency to follow the crowd, which tends to follow the advice of people with seemingly more expertise. These days, it seems that the major push is for investments in equities through no-load mutual funds or ETF's. But you can't necessarily believe what you read or what you are told because your interests may not be the primary concern of the people offering advice.

Much of the advice you hear on television or read in publications is beholden to companies that earn revenue by selling equities. But this often translates into convincing people to take on more risk than they can handle. While there is the potential that everyone will make money when times are good, we've also seen the devastating effects that this can have on retirement savings in recent years.

If the market should crash, the money managers will still earn their 1-2% management fee in a down market. Of course, money managers would much rather make money for their clients because if they are successful, they can attract more investors who will be willing to pay that 1-2% management fee.

The institutions in the markets win as long as they keep their investors, just like how the house always wins as long as gamblers keep gambling. As a result, much of the advice you hear on the Street is tailored towards keeping investors like you in the marketplace. I'm sure you've heard the wisdom that the "market will always come back up" after a downturn. How many times have you been told to "buy and hold"? In a downturn, you'll always hear the money manager claim, "Hey, it was a tough year. Just hold on and it will come back. It always has."

But has it *always* come back?

When the markets were at their peak, there were over 12,000 different mutual funds to invest in. However, with the declines in commissions and the advent of exchange-traded funds (ETFs), mutual funds have gone down in number to around 5,000. If you conduct trend analysis for the next ten years from now, there may be even less than 2,000 mutual funds, as investments in alternative assets continue to grow. So already, we've seen a heavy decline in the mutual fund market that is most likely going to continue.

We saw the markets crash in 2008 and have yet to see them rebound to their original levels, despite years of gradual economic recovery. In August, 2011, we saw volatility that terrified most investors. We've also seen how there is an uncontrollable amount of fraud going on in the marketplace. Civil unrest and natural disasters, like the tsunami/earthquake/nuclear reactor meltdown in Japan, immensely affect the performance of the market. There will always be events that cause the markets to spiral downward and there is no guarantee that markets will rebound even if you wait it out.

Consequently, investing all of your retirement savings in the equity markets, there may be simply too much risk and uncertainty in the marketplace for you to come out on top in the long run, no matter how great the advice you receive. Due to the losses some people experienced in the equity markets, they now can't stop working even though their company wants them gone. Eventually, the companies have to lay off these seasoned employees because of their expense, and those without adequate retirement savings suddenly find themselves in a really hard place.

Yet, there will always be those who believe that they can beat the markets in the long run. They believe they possess more skill and information than the rest of the market. They believe that they can actively time the market and get out before the market takes a downturn. However, no one, no matter how much intuition or information they had, predicted the "flash crash of 2010," the debt ceiling meltdown of Summer, 2011, or the global economic effects of the nuclear disaster from the earthquakes and tsunami in Japan. If somebody could actively time the market a hundred percent of the time, Bill Gates and Warren Buffett would be serving him or her coffee every morning. The reality is that there is no way to predict the behavior of the market in the long run. "Market timing" is really a myth promulgated by those who benefit from people who try to time the market, which are the people who benefit from more trading activity in the marketplace.

But you can make money in the equity markets and still protect your retirement savings if you manage the risks properly. We want to think about the different pools of money we have and treat them differently. As I stated in Chapter 1, you want to have a "guaranteed" pile of money that will maintain your standard of living throughout retirement, and then invest a "maybe" pile of money in the equity markets. These piles are going to be different for everybody. It all depends on how lavish we want our retirement to be and how much we can afford to put at risk.

Kiplinger's Retirement Planning Guide for 2010 said it best: "When deciding how much to invest in an immediate annuity...add up your monthly expenses, subtract any guaranteed sources of income (such as Social Security and pension benefits) and buy an annuity to fill the gap." I think that's one of the most profound sentences I've read in a long time. The editors at Kiplinger's realized that as people go to retire, there might be a problem if the "maybe" pile of money is too large. The only point I differ with Kiplinger's is using an immediate annuity that is irrevocable rather than a deferred annuity that allows you to maintain control and is revocable. Most people prefer control.

Back to the market, if the market cooperates, retirees will get paid, but when it doesn't, they don't get paid. When it comes to retirement, the number one thing people desire is security—they want to get paid.

You can make a lot of money in equities. But you can also lose a lot of money. Remember that the odds always favor the house. The risks involved can come from a plethora of unforeseeable events like computer glitches, natural disasters, rampant fraud, and more!

You also need to be in the business of getting paid. The only way to do this is to set aside the money you need in retirement in something tangible that is guaranteed to provide a steady stream of income for the rest of your life. After you set that money aside and have it work for you, the remaining funds you have left can be used to invest in riskier assets. Any gains you receive on those funds will simply be a bonus since you have all of your needs met. Any catastrophic losses with the riskier assets will not have any material effect on your standard of living in retirement. In Chapter 3, I will explain why many money managers are also turning to this wisdom to attain the consistency they desire in their investments. I will also show how you can set up your own personal pension plan to guarantee the retirement you desire for the rest of your life!

Chapter Three

The Rise of the "DIY Pension Plan"

People often buy too much risk when investing in the equity markets because of the belief that past performance indicates future possibilities. However, if we take a close look at the realities of the past, more often than not you will see that the markets didn't cooperate with every retiree's needs. In order for your retirement to be truly secured, the market must cooperate 100% of the time. But it never has and never will. In fact, the markets have turned downward so dramatically that people have lost over 40% of their portfolio values in recent years. And so, if the world is getting increasingly unstable, why would we base our retirement planning on the rosy expectation that things will only change for the better?

Yet, many people still choose to invest their entire retirement savings in the equity markets. Most of these people are the do-it-yourself types or people that simply trust their brokers' advice. Over the years, I've seen prospective clients come into my office only after they took a devastating loss in the markets. When the dot-com bubble imploded, people were obviously concerned because we had not seen a market correction like that or a pullback as dramatic as that. The market had basically gone up for nearly eighteen years, from 1982 onwards, and so people initially said, "Well, it'll bounce right back." But it didn't. From 2001 to 2003, the market went down every year, and ended up down about 50% after a three-year time period. And some things, particularly in the dot-com sector, lost all of their value.

Then it happened again.

A couple years back, we had the banking fiasco immediately follow the subprime mortgage mess. The markets went down 50% in about six months. We saw the collapse of large financial institutions like Lehman Brothers and Bear Stearns. And again, people were shocked and said, "We thought this was a safe stock." But when it comes to an equity position, even in the blue-chip stocks, stockholders are always the last to get paid. Bondholders will get paid first, preferred stockholders after that, and then if there's any money left, the common stock holder. So if you're last on the food chain in a declining market, should you really be surprised if your value goes to zero?

Of course, some people were hit very hard. This was the second major market correction just within the last decade. So it became apparent our equity investments could go down very far, very fast. That's not an encouraging sign if you're an equity holder who is at or near retirement age. For anyone to take a 50% hit on his or her net worth is absolutely devastating. And if that's right at the time where you need to retire, you have a major problem because you might need to draw on that money. But you can't draw money out of an account that's already underwater because you'll spend that principal down to zero. From a planning perspective, it was truly frustrating to see people come in with $300,000, when a year or two earlier, they were at a million. And they came in saying, "Well, I need $50,000 a year." At that rate, they'll be out of money in six years.

Even more terrifying, the clients who put their money in money markets were not safe either. The money they thought to be safe and liquid turned out to be not safe and not liquid due to concerns of a complete liquidity crisis in the United States. In 2008, the Fed had emergency meetings because the money markets had broken the dollar. So for every dollar you had saved in a money market account, the actual value of the dollar would be less than a dollar. And that's if you could even get your money out. Let's say you had $100,000 saved in a money market account and you wanted to get your money, but every dollar ended up being worth 95 cents. In reality, you would only have $95,000 if you were lucky enough to be able to withdraw it. A few money market funds were completely frozen when people tried to make a withdrawal. You couldn't withdraw any money for a period of time, and when they did finally release it, you only could partial amounts over time. For all practical purposes, it wasn't worth anything because you couldn't get it if you needed it to survive in retirement.

When the money markets broke the dollar, astute financial managers looked at their class portfolios and anybody who had exposure over $100,000 (the maximum amount insured by the government at the time) had that money removed that day. Checks were immediately cut to clients. A total of $87 billion left the financial institutions that day. In cash. $87 billion. In just one day.

The Fed saw that and realized that the amount would be north of a trillion dollars the next day. So they immediately increased the reserves and guaranteed to insure up to $250,000. They pumped all kinds of money into the system. Had the federal government not intervened successfully in 2008, it would have been a run on the banks. It would have been a banking crisis worse than the thirties. And the world would have come to a screeching halt.

So while the dot-com bust simply gave everybody a big haircut, the banking crisis of 2008 threatened to take down the entire economy.

Today, the world is considerably more unstable than it was even three years ago. The American economy has not come back, unemployment is still high, and housing has not come back. Even worse, we've got all this instability in the Middle East and North Africa. Gas prices are skyrocketing. The natural disasters in Japan are forcing American car factories to shut down because they cannot get Japanese parts, and Tokyo could be in rolling blackouts for years. The case against risk is even stronger today than it was in 2008 or 2001.

Many people have decided to just go safe.

After seeing the people in financial peril from too much risk exposure, and the people that were just sitting on a pile of cash, many have developed more perspective. We shifted our focus toward protecting value, especially if clients were at retirement or near retirement. 'Near retirement' being a couple of years from retirement. Because once you *have* enough money, you can say, "I'm okay from here on out, provided I don't lose my savings." So we began to look for strategies that would set up a stream of income in retirement — something that will provide a guaranteed stream of income for life, something like a personal pension plan. In essence, we're going to create our own personal pension plan through fixed indexed annuities. And it (the income) can exist for the rest of your life and your spouse's life. Even more, it can even be a potential inheritance for your beneficiaries.

We have been placing fixed indexed annuities for years now because we figured out a while back that as good as the equity market can be, it will never provide the consistency you need in a retirement plan. As we see the equity markets begin to trend toward these products, more and more people will begin to use them to accomplish their financial goals. We have already seen some 401(k) plans incorporate them into their savings plan. We suspect that very soon, even brokerage firms like Merrill Lynch and Fidelity will be offering fixed index annuities as well because they really are that safe and good.

Even though fixed indexed annuities are one of the best products to build a retirement plan, you still find a lot of resistance and objections to the idea of annuities. Now I'll be the first to admit that fixed indexed annuities are not the sexiest type of investment you can make. You'll never hear guys bragging about how much money they made in a fixed indexed annuity at a cocktail party. People tend to gravitate toward excitement and the thrills of highs and lows. We also love hearing about a great "get rich quick" scheme. It tantalizes our carnal desires for greed and gives us a sense of wonderment and possibility. Fixed indexed annuities, on the other hand, are about as exciting as watching paint dry. But what they are is stable and reliable. You'll get a check in the mail consistently and you'll know exactly what you're going to get. When it comes to retirement income, I think stable and reliable are some of the best qualities you can seek in an investment.

These days, some people will also think it sounds too good to be true. But nearly all the pensions in the world use annuities. Why? *Because they work.* That's why they use them. Social Security is an annuity. Nearly every pension is an annuity. Annuities work because it's income that you can count on. Actuary's methodically crunch numbers to determine what can and cannot be paid out. And since pensions no longer exist, the responsibility lies with individual investors to create their own pension. And they can! And they can do it two ways: one where it is guaranteed and one where it is not. When it's guaranteed, they'll know exactly what they're going to get. When it's not, there's no guarantee to what they're going to get, and so they can get more or they can get less. And they could actually run out of money.

Some people run from annuities because they don't trust insurance companies. I've had people tell me stories of Aunt Sally, who had an insurance policy that she paid regularly for twenty years, and then missed a payment, died and got nothing out of it. I hear all kinds of stories about why insurance companies are bad, but there's a reason these companies have lasted for a few hundred years. They're safe. And they are the creators of this safe money. So you can put your money in the bank and watch it run dry in ten years or less at the current yields, or you can give that money to an insurance company, which will provide a guarantee for the rest of your life.

Others will say that an annuity itself is bad. Somebody might have an Aunt Jane who got an annuity, received payments for one year, died and the money vanished. That is an example of an immediate income with a life only option. Witnessing this unfortunate situation would give somebody a bad taste toward annuities. It would give me a bad taste too. But in this case, Aunt Jane had an immediate annuity, where the principal is gone when the person who possesses the annuity dies. That's not the type of annuity that we suggest people consider. We offer a deferred annuity. So in our case, if Aunt Jane had a million dollars, it would have paid her $5,000 a month. And if she died a year from now, the remaining principal would go directly to her kids. When I educate people about deferred annuities, most people say that they didn't know that this was possible. I normally recommend deferred annuities over immediate annuities because the client can maintain control in a deferred annuity, as opposed to giving up control by giving away the principal in an immediate annuity.

These days, you're not usually looking at Aunt Jane's immediate annuity. A few years ago, the insurance companies realized that baby boomers were retiring, so they set out to redesign annuities. They surveyed large insurance producers like myself and put us together in groups of twenty to fifty people. Then the insurance companies asked us how to design the perfect annuity. When we told them how, they actually listened! They designed what we suggested and that's one of the main reasons why we have this type of deferred annuities today.

The new annuities were redesigned so that instead of annuitizing the money, there would be withdrawals of the money. When you annuitize, you give up control. When you have withdrawals, you maintain control. The insurance companies have always been able to do this, but they were unwilling to do so because more money would go into the investors' pockets. But they had the retiring baby boomers in mind. And they knew that baby boomers want control. They also knew that if they didn't cater to the baby boomers, they would lose out on a large generation of retirees. As a result, the agents offering this product were willing to take a hit in order to gain more business. As a tradeoff for being able to sell this new product with this great feature, our compensation was reduced a fair amount, about 30% or more. But those of us who are in this business for the long term recognize the benefits of having our commission reduced in order to give the clients better, more reliable benefits.

People often say that they're going to wait before creating their pension plans with these annuities. If you want to wait, you can do that. But while you wait, you're at risk of losing 40% of your money in as little as six months. How would you feel if you lost 40% in six months? The Fed may have pumped close to a trillion dollars into the market through its quantitative easing efforts, QE1 and QE2, but if the market goes down 40% again, the chances of a QE3, 4 or 5 happening are pretty slim. The Fed doesn't have another two trillion to pump in. Some people argue that the Fed could print money all day long, and it can, but that will devalue our currency and only cause an even bigger mess. If you already have a sum of money that you've worked hard to acquire and can't afford to lose, then why wait? Protect that money now.

For years, many people have been stubborn about annuities and pension plans. They've said, "I know that the economy has gone up and down, but if I just find the right fund, I'll make 12% a year and I'll be fine."

But the paradigm is shifting.

Retirees and those close to retirement have seen two 50% corrections over a ten-year time period. When I ask people to do the math on their pile of money and figure out how they'd feel if that pile got clipped by 50%, most of them cringe. And most of them have already considered this reality. They just don't know what to do. Nine out of ten people I meet say that protecting their retirement income is exactly what they were looking for. The other 10% of people are the ones who will find a problem with anything.

Another way I keep my clients safe is to ladder their money in fixed annuities and fixed indexed annuities. By 'laddering,' I mean diversifying the term lengths of the hold positions of their annuities with different companies. This way, some annuities mature two years from now, some five years from now, some seven and some ten. I do this to diversify and increase their yields. The tradeoff for liquidity is yield. So in a fixed environment, the longer an annuity is being held, the higher the return should be. That's why I want some short-term, some intermediate and some longer term annuities. Then as money comes due, it gets reinvested at the current rate so we always have money out for the next five to ten years. And because of the improvements in today's annuities, you can now get a higher yield immediately without even giving away the principal.

Most people believe that annuities still only come in one form. They think that if they give a company x number of dollars, then they will get paid $2000 a month until they die, at which point their wife will get only $1000 a month, which will die when she dies. But the annuities that are available today will pay you $2000 a month, and will continue to pay your spouse $2000 a month after you die, and then when your spouse dies, the kids will inherit the leftover principal. This market improvement makes annuities very palatable for people whose biggest knock on annuities was that it used to require that you essentially give away your principal. This is still true of immediate annuities. But you can reclaim control of your money through deferred annuities. And control is the number two thing that retirees want. Number one, of course, is not running out of money.

When I talk with people, I work with each client based on their own financial profile and their attitude toward risk. Just because I play it safe doesn't mean that some clients never play in the stock market, either on their own or with a broker. There are some people who love the stock market, and those people should always have a percentage in it. There are others who don't love the stock market, and in my opinion, they should never be in it. Then somewhere in between lies mostly everybody else.

Hypothetically speaking, if a guy has a half a million dollars and we run an analysis, we might find out that he needs a certain amount of extra income because he has no pension. That extra income could be satisfied with half of that $500,000. So let's say we take $250,000 of his money and create an income stream. He's very happy because all of his income needs are now met, and he's left with $250,000. Then we would probably suggest that he keep about $50,000 to $100,000 of that leftover money liquid. If he keeps $100,000 liquid, he's left with $150,000, which is extra money, and he can do whatever he would like with it. He could even decide to go with a balanced approach of stocks and bonds. So now he has all his income needs met, has liquidity, plus has money situated for growth. Doesn't that sound pretty good?

Other clients with that same starting amount of $500,000 may need $400,000 of that in an income stream. And still others may only need to put $60,000 in. In every case, we solve the income requirements first. Then we always factor in liquidity and solve that. The remaining money after that is what the client could decide to place in the equity markets.

In order to assess a person's income needs and take the first step toward helping him figure out how to pay himself a pension, we begin by doing a fact finder. A fact finder is basically a financial checkup. This assessment helps us ascertain information regarding your banking, your 401(k), your IRAs, your stocks, your bonds, your notes, your real estate, the debt on the real estate, your debt inside the house, your future or current pensions and your future or current Social Security. Basically, it gives us the overall snapshot.

From that snapshot, we put together what's called an asset summary. An asset summary is like a net worth statement, which shows all of your assets on one page. From there, we do an income plan and input your sources of income that we know of such as perhaps a small pension or Social Security or extra rental income. Then we factor in what your accumulated money can produce as an income stream.

In a fact finder, we always ask, "What are the expenditures needed on a monthly basis in retirement?" At this point, we factor in the net amount and also the current tax situation. Then we create an allocation or a proposed blueprint for your retirement.

I prefer to give people options. I show them options A, B and C and tell them that all three will meet their needs, but in different ways depending on how much safe money and money at risk they want.

Most people don't map out their income needs to the extent that we do. We not only factor out the income needs that you will have while you and your wife are both living, but we also factor in what you will need if your spouse dies first and how that could look different if you die first. Then we figure out what that would mean if a death happened today and if it happened five years from now, ten years from now, fifteen, twenty, twenty-five and thirty years from now. Oftentimes, when people consider what the surviving spouse's income will look like, they change their mind about whether they should choose option A as opposed to options B or C.

Most people don't face the fact that upon death, they might have a large drop in income. Let's say a husband has a pension of $50,000 and both he and his wife are making $20,000 a year in Social Security. From just those three income sources, they're at $90,000. But if the husband dies, his wife may lose half his pension and also one of the Social Securities. In this case, we lose $25,000 from the pension and $20,000 from Social Security, which drops the income from $90,000 to $45,000.

Statistically, if you're married and you're 65 or older, there's a 60% chance that either you or your spouse will live for thirty more years. In my seminars, I ask for a show of hands from the married people and then invite them to look at their spouse and determine who that person will be. They always laugh because we all know that some of us aren't going to make it to 95 and some of us will make it there with bells on.

In the scenario just mentioned, let's say the wife lives for another thirty years after the husband dies. Over thirty years, that $45,000 per year that she loses adds up to a loss of $1.35 million. Tack on a Cost of Living Adjustment and we're talking close to two million dollars or even $2.5 million. That's not a small sum of money!

When a couple considers this possibility, it might be suggested that we put together a plan that will kick in an extra $30,000 so that if the husband dies, the income will go from $90,000 to $75,000 instead of $45,000. That would be option B, which takes care of you in case something happens, as opposed to the basic option A. Then option C could put even more money away safely, or it could figure out a way to escrow money so that you can pay $10,000 a year for life insurance.

Developing a game plan for your pension is not something that you will do overnight. It requires several sober conversations, and you'll want to think about it because there are several ways you could map out your retirement income. There are also many different potential problems to solve.

The good news is that people who do not have pension plans can now create their own with the new fixed indexed annuity products now available in the marketplace. And they can create one that will guarantee a stream of income for life, for their life and their spouse's life, plus with a potential inheritance for any beneficiaries. And they can do this all without having to give up control of their saved principal. In my opinion, the newly designed annuity changed the annuity world. It is honestly the best new product I've ever seen in my career. And as I've said before, its positive repercussions will be enormous over the next several years.

So that's how you take care of your own pension. But what about those around you? What do you do for them, when, as the expression goes, you're out of the picture? I know it's unpleasant to think about. But what's even more unpleasant is what happens to our loved ones if we don't take care of them while we're still here. How to do that is the subject of the next chapter.

Chapter Four

Leaving a Financial Legacy

There's a story about the man lying on his deathbed who smells his wife's delicious apple pie cooling on the kitchen counter. Feebly, he says, "Before I go, could I possibly have one more slice of that wonderful pie?"

"No," says his wife. "That's for *after.*"

Okay—no pie for us! But what are providing our loved ones for… *after?*

By now, we've ensured that we will have a secure, stable retirement with our personal pension plans. We've talked about how we can ladder fixed indexed annuities to create our personal pension plans. In this chapter, I want to show you how to leave a positive financial legacy for those you love. In other words, we'll discuss how the pension plan you create can outlive you!

Like most people, you want to secure the financial future for your loved ones when you are no longer around. Many people who come into my office do not like to discuss these things. It's perfectly understandable. No one likes to talk about death. But we really do need to think about and plan for these things because nobody lives forever.

I can't stress enough about how important it is to take the necessary precautions while you are still alive to ensure that your loved ones are cared for after you pass. In this chapter, we'll focus on how to set things up so that the hard work you invest in a solid financial plan will pay off into perpetuity: for your spouse, for your children, and for your loved ones.

Most people do not realize that there are a number of financial problems that can arise after death. Assets need to be transferred. Stocks may need to be re-registered. The estate might have to go through a probate. So the more you plan before you pass, the easier it will be for your loved ones to be provided for afterwards. It is always better to be proactive about financial planning as opposed to reactive. Having a good plan in place before you die will provide you and your loved ones peace of mind. And when dealing with the loss of a loved one, sometimes the financial aspects surrounding death are the last things that a loved one wants to think about. There is a tremendous amount of grief and shock that surrounds the loss of a loved one, so having a plan in place eliminates a lot of the mistakes that are sometimes made under duress.

Let's look at an example to see the material impact that may arise from a death. And then we'll look at the solutions that financial planners take to minimize the subsequent financial loss that often arises after someone passes away.

Let's take Bob. He's 72 years old and retired. His Social Security income is $24,000 a year. Let's say Bob has a wife, Sally, who is 68, and also has a Social Security income of about $12,000 a year. Together, Bob and his wife have a total income of $36,000 a year. Maybe that's enough for them to live on. But now let's say Bob passes away, and Sally has the choice to take the higher of the two Social Security incomes. So her Social Security income would now be $24,000 a year, but she will lose her own $12,000 a year Social Security. So now, her household income is $24,000 as opposed to $36,000. That's a big drop in income! She will lose a third of her income that she depends on in retirement.

If Bob and Sally talk to a financial planner who works with retirees, the planner would ask them to estimate how much they need to survive in retirement. Let's say that they need the full $36,000 to live on in retirement. So everything is fine unless Bob or even Sally passes away. When one of them dies, they will lose $12,000 a year in Social Security. So the planner would probably recommend that they set up a side fund that kicks in an extra $12,000 a year when Bob kicks out. There are a number of factors that determine how much they need to put in that side fund, but let's say that have to put $200,000 into a side fund (fixed indexed annuity with a guaranteed income benefit rider) in order to generate $12,000 a year, two or three years down the line. If they do that, Bob and Sally would be protected in the event that either one of them passes away.

The same recommendation can be made when it comes to that side fund as it is with the personal pension plan. The reason is this: even though Bob and Sally have secured their retirement while they are both alive, the moment one of them passes, the surviving spouse instantly is underwater and does not have enough to make ends meet. So that's a lot of risk that arises from one tragic event. But that risk can be mitigated if that surviving spouse can generate $12,000 from another stream of protected income. And because the livelihood of the surviving spouse is at stake, we want to make sure this side fund is also generated from a safe investment that is guaranteed.

This is why. Let's say Bob and Sally have $250,000 of investment assets. They might have $50,000 saved in a CD at a bank, and let's say they have the remaining $200,000 in something that has a lot of risk associated with it. Even though their retirement is guaranteed and secured while both Bob and Sally are still alive, if Bob dies and the $200,000 is now worth substantially less. Sally will still need the $12,000 a year in retirement. So, she is going to take that $12,000 a year out to live on, but what if the at risk money is only worth $100,000. When she takes that $12,000 out of that account, she is left with $88,000. So that's even less money that she has to rebuild or invest with.

With people like Bob and Sally, I would ask them if they want to set up a plan where they know without a doubt that Sally will have enough money coming in regardless of what the markets do or don't do. This is a type of survivorship planning because their retirements are already secured through Social Security.

So now, we would plan to make sure that the surviving spouse is provided for in the event that someone passes. In my survivorship planning, it may be recommend that they exit risk and protect that money. Another solution is to use a life insurance policy to make sure that Sally is provided for when Bob dies. They could take out a life insurance policy that is worth $200,000 and place those proceeds in an annuity to generate the additional $12,000 that Sally will lose when Bob passes. However, another important consideration that we need to think about is if Bob, at age 72, doesn't already have life insurance, he is probably not going to purchase it because it is going to cost them a fair amount of money. If Bob has lots of assets, he might be able to afford the premiums, but if he doesn't, I am not sure he is going to afford $10,000 a year to buy a $200,000 policy.

When it comes to survivorship planning, there is also an equally strong tendency to return to the equity markets. People often are more willing to take bigger risks because they feel comfortable that retirement is secured. I've seen this more often in men. Men tend to take bigger risks and are often prone to keeping money in the stock market until age 80. At age 80, they become a little more risk averse and feel more fallible. But before then, men always feel that they are in charge and that they make all the right decisions.

But I can't tell you how many times I have seen clients make the exact wrong choices, in retirement planning and in survivorship planning as well. Even if we are comfortable with assuming some risk, there is a right way to do it and a wrong way to do it. Far too often, I have seen people assume way too much risk in the equity markets. This is especially true if they feel a sense of security in retirement.

Too many times, I have seen people invest far too much money on one individual stock. Many people will have more of a tendency to do that with their "maybe" pile of money. They think that it should be fine because it is a blue chip stock that will, as they believe, "never go down in value." And even if it goes down, it will not go down that much. When they think about how much their spouse will need after they pass away, they believe the surviving spouse will be able to live off the dividends of that stock. Well, the reality is that dividends can be slashed and stock prices can go way, way down. We saw this in 2008. So, if we go back to our example of Bob and Sally, Sally needs $12,000 a year from the assets they have after Bob passes away. No matter what, Sally has to cash out $12,000 of the assets each year. So even if they are secured in their retirement right now, the moment Bob passes away, Sally will run out of money in retirement, particularly if the markets are declining in value. It is mathematical fact if the markets are not cooperative.

So you never want to have all of your eggs in one basket. Any common stock can go down in value. And it could go down for any number of reasons. All it takes is one investigation by the federal government on the company's accounting practices, or an attempt to break up the company because the government thinks the company is acting like a monopoly. It happened to Microsoft and Ma Bell. Or look at supposedly "safe" stocks of the recent past: GM or Lehman Brothers. And when a company goes down in value, it can stay down for many, many years.

A lot of people stay in the markets because of the overriding belief that markets will always go back up. They are more inclined to take on risk when it is money that they feel they do not need immediately. If they have Social Security income and a pension plan for retirement, they may feel more inclined to take a loss. But you have to remember what type of return you need to earn in order to make up for any realized losses you suffer. If the stock market goes down 50%, what type of return do you need to earn to get back to where you started? Many people simply believe they need to earn back 50% to make them whole. But, the answer is really a 100% return. So if you do take a loss, you need to work twice as hard just to get back to where it was. Knowing this, if you knew you had to draw on this money in a few short years, would you still be willing to take on that risk?

Now, you might be thinking that the market has already doubled from its lowest point in 2008. But if you actually look at a lot of people's accounts, their accounts are still lower than they were a couple of years back. The market might be up, but there is no guarantee that you will be. If you look at most mutual funds, 85% do worse than the S&P 500 in the up years, and they do worse than the S&P 500 in the down years. So, the reality is that most mutual funds and most investment accounts don't capture all the gains the market makes, and they lose more money than the market overall.

There will always be various motivations for people to try their luck in the stock market. Sometimes people think that if they put $200,000 in the stock market, they might be able to generate $14,000 a year, instead of the $12,000 a year they'll get from putting the $200,000 in an annuity. But you have to ask yourself if you really want that extra $2,000. Some might say yes. But is that extra $2,000 really worth the risk of running out of money in retirement if all of a sudden you or your spouse needs that money in a few years because you or your spouse passes away?

There are also those people who are willing to indulge in "short term" risk, especially with the markets recovering right now. They'll invest the extra $200,000 and say, "I am going to ride my losses and sell when the Dow gets back to 14,000." But then the Dow gets to 14,000 and what happens next? Analysts will start saying that we are going to hit new highs, the market will go way up, and so people will recalibrate their limits to 16,000 or 18,000. They'll continue justifying the risks involved until the market crashes. And when the market crashes and they suddenly need that money because a spouse dies, that's when any security they had in retirement dissolves.

When it comes to survivorship planning, it also troubles me when I hear people say, "Well, she can always sell the house." That is simply not the case anymore with housing prices down significantly in value throughout the United States. If you have to do a forced sale in order to survive in retirement, you might take a substantial discount off of an already low price. So, let's say your house may have hit $600,000 at its peak, but today, it is worth $400,000. If you have a year or two to wait, you might get be able to get the full $400,000. But you need to sell it now to use that money in retirement, so you'll probably only get $300,000. Now, that is a 50% loss that your spouse will take. And if you made the calculation that your spouse could live off the $600,000 value of the house, and there is only $300,000 from the sale, that is a serious problem! We either have to lower our expectation of what those proceeds could generate or we have to die before the money dies.

We have to remember that there is a false sense of security if our retirement plan relies on streams of income from two people. If you need to rely on income from your spouse to make your retirement plan work, then you need to plan in the event that you or your spouse passes away. That is proper survivorship planning. And this planning is no different than creating our personal pension plans because this will be money that we will rely on in retirement.

When people lose the love of their lives with whom they spent 30, 40, or 50 years, they may be in a state of mind where they can't figure things out. So the smartest thing you can do to protect your loved ones and protect your personal pension plan is to find a financial services professional who is an expert on survivorship planning. You want someone who can walk you through the process of what needs to be done in preparation and someone who can guide your surviving loved ones through the difficult period with regard to these financial matters. Now, I am sure you can put together a will or a trust on the Internet and find instructions on what to do, but most people generally don't know what to do, particularly after going through a traumatic incident like a death in the family.

I would always suggest getting professional help as it relates to your money — you don't want to suffer catastrophic loss from any mistakes. I highly recommend against the do-it-yourself method because it is like preparing your own taxes or defending yourself in a court without an attorney. This is your money and potentially the livelihood of you and your loved ones. It always helps to have someone that is versed on the topics that you need help with.

When I discuss retirement planning with my clients, we always map out the client's assets with their own asset summary. Then we map out their current sources of income, and any income they'll continue or expect to receive the rest of their lives. Lastly, we also factor what if the client dies first or if their spouse dies first. We'll develop scenarios of what might happen if the death happens 5, 10, 15, 20,

25, and 30 years from now. This allows them to see in black and white exactly what their income needs really are. From a planning standpoint, we always want to meet the client's income needs. Then we'll go over the main survivorship plan and factoring in how much risk we are willing to take. Most people over retirement do not want to take too much risk.

So when you meet with someone, you want to make sure they know how to set up an income plan for life in retirement. Your professional should factor in how much income you absolutely need to pay your bills. Once you protect that base amount of income, you are pretty much set. Now, some professionals might recommend returning to the equity markets to combat the effects of inflation. After all, many publications do say the way you combat inflation is with stocks because that is the only place you will get above inflation return. That could be a double-edged sword. While all of that may be true over time, it may not be time-sensitive to you because of your life expectancy. In other words, the market may well come back and hit new highs...but will you be here to see it?

So a word caution might be prudent when it comes to that kind of thinking. From a planning standpoint, if I just protect more money in the savings account, I can protect the baseline income and give my clients a raise each year in retirement with safe money as opposed to risky money.

When we prepare our clients for survivorship planning, we always try to make sure that they are prepared in the event of death, and that any transfer of benefits is seamless and as easy as possible. This is often a difficult period in a person's life and any stress from financial burdens will always make things worse. I always recommend taking a proactive approach and in our firm, we put together a personal financial inventory binder that covers all of our client's financial documents.

Documents such as: their IRAs, their 401(k)s, their pensions, their Social Security, any life insurance or long-term care. Sometimes, we would even include their will or their trust. If they work with estate planning attorneys, they may have a separate binder just for that. We put it all in a personal financial inventory binder and then monitor it on an annual basis. So if something happens to one of the parties, the surviving spouse knows exactly where to go. They would generally contact us and say there has been a death in the family. We then walk them through the necessary steps to retitle assets, or make sure the beneficiary's designations get executed the way they should.

I really can't stress how important it is to get all these things done ahead of time. Knowing it is done correctly will ensure a smooth transition to the husband, the wife, or even the kids. I can't tell you the number of times people have come to me after a tragic death, and in some cases, it'll take a year or longer to retitle assets or get through probate. Somebody might even step in and challenge it, thus creating even more delay. In the meantime, the surviving member might need money, but everything is tied up in the courts. It's really a heartbreaking situation. But these are real things that happen every single day.

And after the survivorship plan is in place, if a death does happen, the surviving spouse will also need to come in and do the necessary updates to their plans, like retitling assets, updating transfer-on-death accounts, or adding additional beneficiaries to the forms. For example, let's say my wife was the beneficiary of my account, but now she predeceased me. I'll need to put a new primary beneficiary because if I leave it the same way and I die, the money will go to her estate, which is the absolute worst thing that could happen, as any trust attorney will tell you.

So it is important to make sure all these things are in place and that you have planned it all out. If you are going to work your entire life to ensure that you secure in your retirement, it is just as important to leave your loved ones with the same security that you enjoy. By creating a clear survivorship plan, you can ensure that you leave a strong financial legacy that will provide for the people you care for most, even when you are no longer around. This all might seem complicated, but it is actually a really simple process for someone well-versed in it because they have done it a number of times. There is really no substitute for experience. And once you do have it all in place, you will truly have the security and peace of mind of knowing that both you and your loved ones are provided for during and even after your retirement.

Chapter Five

Leveraging Your Life Insurance

When most people think about life insurance, and they think about it as infrequently as possible, they're really thinking about it as "death insurance." If they die, which they won't, of course, but if they do, their survivors get a big chunk of cash. And that's the alpha and the omega of life insurance in most people's minds—I die, she gets paid.

But there's so much more to it than that when you're thinking about creating your own pension and taking care of those you love. That's what we'll discuss right now.

Life insurance can be a very powerful tool in ensuring the perpetuity of your personal pension plan. When we talk about survivorship planning, life insurance can often be used to supplement any loss of income streams you may lose when a spouse passes away. In addition, life insurance can also be used to multiply any retirement savings you may have and pass on the fruits of your lifetime of labor to future generations, like your grandchildren. Of course, with any type of retirement planning, it always helps to start early and purchasing the right kind of life insurance is no exception. As you get older, life insurance premiums will likely increase exponentially as you become more of a liability for payout. In addition, you may not qualify for certain types of life insurance as you get older. There is an old Chinese aphorism that goes, "The best time to plant a tree was 20 years ago. The second best time is now." The same concept applies towards life insurance.

In this chapter, I'll show you how you can use life insurance to leverage your retirement savings after you pass away. I'll also demonstrate how life insurance can be a great tool in survivorship planning, particularly if you haven't saved enough to supplement any income streams you might lose when someone passes. We will go over the various types of life insurance available and I'll show you how you can use existing income streams to cover the cost of insurance premiums. I'll also demonstrate to you why adding life insurance premium on to your cost of retirement is absolutely worth the added expense.

There are two basic types of life insurance: term and permanent. Term life insurance is temporary and you usually purchase it for a fixed amount of time, say 5, 10, 15, or 20 years. Because the coverage is temporary, the cost is often cheaper. Permanent, universal life or whole life, insurance covers you for the rest of your life. Consequently, the premiums for permanent life insurance are much more costly. Still, there are different advantages in using both products to achieve the investment objectives of our clients. It all depends on what are our clients' specific needs for that life insurance.

Let's say a couple is retiring soon. The wife is younger than the husband, so we still have eight years before the wife's Social Security of $20,000 a year kicks in. Let's also say we still have a mortgage that costs $20,000 a year and let's say that the mortgage will be paid off in 8 years. If something were to happen to the husband, she might be in a difficult spot because her Social Security will not start for another eight years and there's still debt on the house. So we would recommend that the couple buy a term policy that lasts at least 8 years, generally 10 years. Now if something were to happen, she would be protected financially from the loss of her husband.

Most people, if they understood life insurance, would prefer permanent because their purpose for having life insurance is to be in place when they die. Many people believe that life insurance is more important while they were raising a family, paying for the house, and saving for retirement. They believe that life insurance is primarily a means of income replacement. But as they get older, the kids grow up, the house is paid off, and they get closer to retirement, many say, "You know, I don't need any income replacement anymore. So, why would I spend money on life insurance?"

This might be a true statement, or it might be a little shortsighted. Let's take a deeper look.

Most public pensions do not have a 100% survivor benefit. For the most part, the majority of them get reduced by approximately 50%. In addition, if both the husband and wife have Social Security, we are going to lose some Social Security income when one of them passes. So life insurance can be the perfect vehicle to replace a loss of income with a bucket of tax-free money. This money could then be used to generate the lost income stream that might arise from the loss of a spouse. Even more, life insurance may be an even more powerful vehicle to accomplish certain financial objectives because of leverage.

Let's say that I am a 65-year-old male in average health. I can buy $250,000 permanent universal life policy for $6,400 a year. So let's say I make one payment $6,400, and then I die tomorrow. My spouse would get $250,000 tax-free! Now that would be a tremendous invest-ment of $6,400. (And bad luck for me.) So if we take that $250,000 insurance payment and set it up into an income stream for my spouse, she could generate $12,500 a year for the rest of her life without ever touching the principal! That's fantastic! And we would get all of this from simply paying in one $6,400 premium. There's really no other vehicle that has ever been created that works like life insurance.

We're currently seeing a major comeback in life insurance. I believe there are two primary reasons why this is happening.

The first reason why there has been an uptick in the sales of life insurance has to do with people aged 70 and a half or older. Many Americans have IRA accounts. When you have an IRA, at age 70 and a half, you have to start taking out a required minimum distribution. It's a mandatory requirement that will result in a 50% penalty if you don't follow it. And you still have to pay tax on the minimum distribution amount regardless of whether or not you take it. So, all retirees with IRA accounts are going to take the required minimum distribution at age 70 and a half.

As an example, let's say we have a client age 70 ½ with $400,000 in their IRA account. They have to take out a required minimum distribution of $14,705. Now, let's say they have other retirement income streams set up, so they don't need that $14,705. In this scenario, we would suggest that they take $12,000 of that and buy a life insurance policy. The reason why we only use $12,000 is because we have to pay $2,705 in taxes on the distribution. This is for someone whose effective tax rate is about 20%. So, after we hold out money for taxes, we take the balance and see what kind of life insurance we could buy. Usually for $12,000 in premiums a year, I can buy about a $400,000 tax-free permanent death benefit. So essentially, we have taken our $400,000 IRA asset and leveraged it to be worth nearly $800,000 ($400,000 from the IRA and $400,000 from the life insurance policy). So, when the client passes away, the $400,000 IRA is still taxable, but the life insurance is tax-free. That's fantastic! So, a lot of people are now creating a bigger estate where one might not exist. And they are doing it with life insurance.

Better still, people are using that $400,000 in retirement savings to get an annuity that would generate the life insurance premium for the rest of their lives. And when the person passes, there will still be a balance in the annuity and the surviving spouse will have the life insurance payment. You could see how powerful this is when people say they might need that extra $400,000 of tax-free dollars to help generate some income for the surviving spouse or maybe even pass on to some grandchildren for their college savings plan. Wouldn't that be great if you had four grandchildren and you can leave each one with $100,000 income tax-free. It's tremendous! I know I sound very excited about…life insurance. Okay. That's because I'm a financial guy and I have witnessed firsthand the tremendous benefits for those families that were properly insured. What I'm really excited about is the way life insurance provides for people's financial futures at a relatively low cost.

The second reason why life insurance sales have gone up is due to the people who have pensions or people that would like to create one. Here's an example that we see every day in our firm:

You have a 65-year-old retired federal employee with an $80,000 a year government pension. Now, he doesn't have Social Security because he has the federal pension. The survivor benefit on that $80,000 is 55%, so if the federal employee dies, his spouse would get $44,000 a year.

Now, let's say his spouse works, but didn't have a pension. Instead, the wife has saved $300,000 in IRA money and she is entitled to $20,000 a year in Social Security. Let's imagine the wife to be 62-years-old. So, they are both retired and their retirement income stream is $100,000, without her touching her $300,000 IRA. Now let's say that her $300,000 IRA could generate $12,000 a year guaranteed.

If something happens to him, they are going to lose $36,000 a year because his pension will be reduced by 45%. So, she could experience a drop of this income from $100,000 down to $64,000. But if I took her $12,000 from the IRA and use it to buy life insurance, I could buy about a $400,000 life insurance policy on him. That $400,000 payment if he dies down the road could generate about $20,000 a year.

So, in the event that the husband passes and there is a reduction in the pension payment, she still keeps her social security, but now she has $20,000 coming in from the proceeds on the life insurance, as well as the $12,000 coming in from her IRA. Now, you might stop and say her IRA was set up to pay the premium for the life insurance. But the life insurance was on his life, when he's gone; she no longer has to pay it. Thus, we have a total of $64,000 plus $20,000, along with $12,000. So that's still roughly $96,000 of income in retirement even when he's gone. Isn't that pretty good?

Basically, we can use life insurance to recreate the pensions that you will lose in the event of somebody passing. It's definitely the most cost-effective way possible, and, in most cases, it's the only way possible. Of course, all this is under the assumption that the individual can qualify for life insurance. Most life insurance policies require a physical and a blood/urine test that would have to be taken to make sure they are eligible. But if they are eligible, and we have the resources to do it, it makes perfect sense.

However, sometimes people are still very resistant to the idea of life insurance. They often don't want to pay for the added expense in retirement. They often do not want to spend that money because it's so intangible. They don't think they're getting anything from it. And they don't want to think about dying. So I'll often try to illustrate why protecting their retirement income streams after they pass away is actually quite sensible. I'll put it all into perspective by working the numbers for them.

Sometimes, we have people with pensions substantially above the numbers we used as examples. So in order to show them how important it is to protect that income stream, I try and equate their pension income with an amount of money that they would have to have in a side fund to recreate their pension. As an example, one of my clients is starting retirement pension that is $150,000 a year with a cost of living adjustment. So, if he lives a long time, that pension could get up to $300,000 a year. How much would he have to have in an annuity today to recreate that pension? The answer is between $4 and $5 million. Now that's a *lot* of money.

It's actually a ton of money since this particular client was only 60-years-old at the time. So, what I might say to that individual is, "Why don't we protect a million dollars of that, or let me just preserve two million of that?" That would cost about him about $35,000 a year to protect two million dollars. Now most people would say that $35,000 a year seems a little high to pay for life insurance premiums. And I'll refer back to the four or five million dollars that I would need to have in a side fund to create that stream of income.

In most of these cases, the person has the $150,000 pension and other income streams as well. They usually won't even need the $150,000. They'll only need a portion of it. So, I'll say to them, "Why don't I slice off 20% of it and create a pension that outlives you?" They might ask why they'll need to do that. I'll then illustrate why spending money on life insurance is actually preserving their wealth.

For this pension guy, he could be one of two things: he could be single or he could be married. For the single guy, if he dies the next day, no money goes to anybody. The pension dies when he dies. If he was married at the time of his passing, his spouse would get $82,500 a year for the rest of her life. But suppose his spouse only lives 5 or 10 years longer. This guy worked his tail off for his entire life to get a pension that is worth several millions of dollars, but if he doesn't live, all that money goes back to company or, in this case, the federal government. So, what we tell him is that if he really wants to capture and protect the wealth he has earned, we should shave off 10%, 20%, or 30% of the pension and reposition that into life insurance.

Now, he might still say that's a lot of money. The $35,000 a year insurance premium is not small change. And that's when I'll work the numbers further to show him the comparative value.

Ten years from now with just a 2% cost of living adjustment, his income will be $182,000. Twenty years from now with just a 2% cost of living adjustment, his income will be $222,000. Now, let's say the guy has a 20 year life expectancy, so his average income between now to the time he dies will be $182,000 just from his pension alone. So, if we are only paying $35,000 in premium, we are essentially letting the cost of living adjustment pay for the premium! So, my point is this: if he dies 10 years from now and he's a single person, the $182,000 is completely gone he has nothing to show for his life's work and his beneficiaries get nothing. But if he follows my plan and spends the $35,000 on premiums, his beneficiaries would get two million dollars of tax-free money. He would leave a huge financial legacy behind for all of his years of hard work.

Most people who collect a pension are savers of that pension money. They will not spend all of that money. So I often tell them, "If you are not going to spend all that money, why don't we leverage some of that into a life insurance policy." Now I can't buy $5 million policy, even though that's what I would need if I really wanted to capture all the wealth from that pension. But I can capture 25% to 50% of it by purchasing a one to two million dollar insurance policy.

When it's properly presented, people love it. I'll also tell them that pensions will not exist like this in the future. So, their children and their grandchildren are going to need a lot more money. They are really going to have to save their money. But how much are they going to save? In order for them to have enough to maintain the same standard of living that the pension provides, they'll have to save $5 million. What is the likelihood their children could each save and accumulate $5 million in their lifetimes?

The chances are pretty slim.

But if you could start the 3 children with $750,000 in tax-free dollars, isn't that a great head start?

Absolutely!

Yet, many people still do not utilize life insurance policies because they don't think they can get it, they don't understand it, or more importantly, they are worried about how they will pay the premium. But when you can show them how the premium can be paid from another guaranteed vehicle, it reduces a lot of their anxiety.

Other times, people might have preconceived notions about life insurance policies. Some might say, "I remember my Aunt Sally paying on a policy. She made some payments. She died and the company didn't pay her beneficiaries because it was a whole life policy that was front-loaded. They might not have kept it long enough for it to pay for itself, so they lost their premiums." In many front-loaded policies, it takes longer for the policy to break even, usually around fifteen to twenty years. But once the policy breaks even, it becomes a cash cow. But if you have to eat the cow before it becomes a cash cow, you will be out of life insurance and out of money. So it really is about finding the right product to meet your needs as well. Not everybody makes the right decision with their money, but our clients usually do. We have protected a lot of our client's wealth.

Other objections may stem from the recent lack of trust for Wall Street and insurance companies like AIG. But I believe most insurance companies are being wrongly tarred with the same brush. I don't believe it's really warranted. Insurance companies, for the most part, have been in business longer than any other institutions in the United States. One such company our firm does business with was founded back in the late-1600s, and is the oldest, continuous insurance company in the world. When you are an old company, you've stuck around by doing the right things. Even though the New York Stock Exchange has been around for more than 200 years, the companies listed on the exchange simply have not been around that long. They don't last. Companies go through cycles. The companies may morph into something else, but they don't last. So there's a reason why the insurance companies I favor have been around a century or more. They are doing the right thing: they are not taking a lot of risk.

Life insurance rates have never been cheaper than they are now. They are the lowest that it has ever been because life expectancy is increasing. People are living longer. So the premiums for new policies are really starting to come down now. It's come to the point where it is much more affordable than people think. So I would tell the people wavering around the fence about whether to do this to simply do it now. When it comes to life insurance the only thing that can happen by waiting is bad or not favorable.

Generally, we don't get in better health as we age. The actuarial tables don't improve as we get older. So, if we are eligible today, take advantage of it especially if you have the money to do it. A number of these policies can be accessed prior to death for long-term care or terminal illness stays, so if I have a policy for a million or 10 million dollars, depending on the carrier, I may be able to access 20% to 50%, and in some cases, 90% to 100% of whatever the death benefit is prior to my passing. Now that's really fantastic! Insurance companies really figured out what people want and need.

You really don't want to wait, particularly with term insurance—because term insurance is temporary. I had a 74-year-old man come into my office the other day trying to buy some term life insurance for 20 years. I couldn't help but start to chuckle. When he asked me what was so funny, I told him that nobody is going to write a term life insurance on a 74-year-old man for a 20-year term. He asked, "Why not?" So I told him because his life expectancy is 78 to 80 years and the actuaries think he'll be dead long before the policy expires. I then suggested that he go with a permanent policy, but the premiums are going to be much more because they know they can charge a higher premium since you are older and you are approaching your life expectancy.

So people often think they can buy term life forever, but they can't. So you should really try to buy a bigger term policy when you are younger, can afford it, and still can actually get it. Or you should look into a permanent plan.

A lot of people might not want anything that is going to cut into their consumption lifestyle. I truly understand this. This is the main reason why we often offer solutions to fund the premiums through alternative streams of income. Or they might not want to think about dying. But the reality is that you need to think about your consumption-based lifestyle versus the long-term needs that you have in order to take care of yourself and your loved ones. Because when you are gone, will their needs or desires for the consumption lifestyle end?

Probably not.

So, when you plan properly with life insurance, you are really protecting that as well. But if you don't plan, their consumption requirements are going to have to go down. So, you really want to do some planning with a planner who is creative and can show you how to protect your wealth without sacrificing your retirement lifestyle. That's what we do at my firm. When we show our plans to our clients, they usually tell us, "That's what I want right there!"

As a last example, I recently had a case where I had a client saving $10,000 a month after tax. That's after his bills are paid, after his taxes are paid, he's just got a lot of money coming in and wants to see what else can we do. I immediately said, "Let's take $4,000 of that and create a tax-free bucket of money." At the time, we thought we could write a policy that was close to a million dollars, but we ended up doing about $725,000. The main reason was he wasn't in perfect health. But this individual is about 76 or 77 years of age. So, when he passes, in addition to the other wealth that he has accumulated, I'm going to give his wife or the kids an additional $725,000 tax-free, just from $4,000 a month for the next couple of years.

At some point, it's just plain old common sense. It really is a no-brainer. With the right life insurance policy, you can leverage your current income streams to not only provide additional income for what your spouse may lose after you pass, but also an exponentially larger financial legacy for your beneficiaries. You can give them a great head start for your family and for your heirs as well. It really is a perfect solution!

Chapter Six

What About Your Health?

As we age during retirement, our expenditures might rise due to deteriorating health conditions and rising health care costs. When this happens, we will quickly find that our income needs will increase significantly. So far in this book, we've already talked about how we can secure ourselves financially through our own personal pension plan in retirement. Then we talked about how we can set up a plan to continue to take care of our spouse and heirs even after we pass away. We also explored various options of setting up side funds and life insurance policies to ensure the financial stability of our beneficiaries. But life is often unpredictable, and one of the most devastating threats to a solid financial plan in retirement is the rising cost of long-term care. In this chapter, we'll discuss one of the best ways to mitigate these risks: supplementing your retirement income with long-term care insurance.

In the United States, if you have money and you get sick when you're older, to the extent that you need skilled nursing care, you have to spend your own money to receive that care. If you don't have enough money, then you will deplete the funds that you have and then it'll be the state's turn to take care of you. The point of long-term care insurance is to prevent this from happening and protect your assets from spend-down.

Let's say that someone has $800,000 of investment assets, which includes everything in the bank, everything in annuities and other funds. Then let's say that this person gets sick and finds out that $300,000 of that money now has to be allocated toward healthcare. Now, if this person passes away, the surviving spouse will have significantly less savings with which to generate an income stream.

There is also the chance that the person in this example could end up in a nursing care facility for an extended period of time. The average stay in a facility is about three years or less, but with Alzheimer's or Parkinson's disease, that stay could last substantially longer. This person could be at the facility for ten years! If a long-term care policy were in place, it would help keep this person's assets intact potentially forever or for the rest of his life no matter how sick he gets and no matter from where he ends up needing to receive care.

The approach I prefer is a combination of both life insurance and long-term care insurance. This plan is more than likely the way that most people will choose to take care of their long-term care planning over the next few years. Because of this combination, several of the large insurance carriers have experienced a forty percent rate increase, which they have passed along to their clients. The highlight that draws most people to this combination of life with long-term care is that the premium can never increase.

The combination works like this: let's say that a man buys a $300,000 death benefit. He can access two percent each month, which is $6,000 a month, and pull that out from his life and long-term care insurance combination on a tax-free basis if he is in a facility or if he's receiving treatment at home through a licensed professional. The premiums on this plan are age dependent and it has to go through underwriting, but let's say that the premium in this scenario is $8,000. With a traditional long-term care insurance plan, the same person could spend a little bit less, maybe $6,000 a year, on a long-term care insurance plan, but if he died 15 years from now, his beneficiaries wouldn't get any money. Basically, if he goes the traditional route without the combination, the person would pay $90,000 into the plan, but would never get any use out of it if he dies instead of needing long-term care. Yes, that plan would protect what it needed to protect. If he gets sick, his care and facility costs would be covered. But there would be no bump or no proceeds for the beneficiaries. The life and long-term care combination might cost a little bit more each month, but you would get the death benefit associated with it. So whatever you don't spend down in long-term care would be paid out later as a death benefit free of income tax.

The underwriting for the life and long-term care combination plan isn't much more complicated than the typical medical underwriting that goes along with regular life insurance policies. The long-term care portion has the potential to be a bit trickier if somebody has preexisting conditions that indicate that possible long-term care is not too far away. Examples of people with pre-existing conditions include somebody who uses a walker or somebody who has already been diagnosed with a mild form of dementia or somebody who has already been diagnosed with another disease such as Parkinson's. Some pre-existing conditions are outright declinations for the long term care component of the plan. It's not impossible to get you covered if you have any pre-existing conditions, but the underwriting process can be much more difficult.

When the insurance company is on the hook to pay out your long-term care benefits, they abide by the definition of long-term care as defined in the contract that you first signed. The contract generally states that when two or more "activities of daily living" are present, you're eligible to receive payment. Activities of daily living are defined as the things that we normally do, which include bathing, eating, dressing, maintaining continence by controlling the bladder or taking care of personal hygiene, getting to and from the toilet and being ambulatory.

After the insurance company determines that two or more of the activities of daily living are present, then they follow the elimination period you established in the contract. You could have selected a 0-day waiting period, which means that your payments begin immediately, but you could have also chosen a 100-day or 180-day wait. If you selected a longer waiting period, then for those first 100 days or 180 days, you have to self-fund your care costs, which could cost quite a bit of money depending on your needs. There is also the possibility that Medicare could pay for a portion of your first 80-100 days, but that depends on certain very strict definitions of long-term care that they've established. After the given amount of days that Medicare helps you, however, it stops paying you regardless of whether or not you're still stuck in your insurance company's waiting period.

Think about long-term care insurance from a demographic standpoint. Today, we have such a surge in life expectancy that many people anticipate that they might spend almost thirty years in retirement. In the old days, when somebody stopped working, they died not too long afterward. Three years in retirement is significantly less than the nearly three decades of retirement that people look forward to today. The one drawback about living longer is that if you do eventually need the assistance of a nursing facility, that long-term care could become an even longer-term care. And there's no way to predict that.

Here are your options: *you can either pay a relatively small amount now for long-term care insurance, or you can spend a whole lot later on your healthcare.* But if you choose to take the risk of having to spend down your assets on long-term care in the future, remember that that's the money you could have used for your grandchildren or your spouse or for maintaining your quality of life. Whether you pay now or pay later, you will pay either way. But I guarantee that with a stable long-term care insurance plan in place, you will be paying a lot less if you pay now.

There are several payment options for long-term care insurance plans. Many companies offer a triple option. This is where we can make a single premium payment into a life insurance contract that also has a long-term care, and also operates similarly to an annuity. This option covers all of your bases, but there are lots of different options available to fit your particular needs. The key to choosing an option is to sit down with a professional that works in this field and knows what they're doing. That professional will help you design a plan that will protect you and your loved ones. As long as you talk to somebody who has done this work for a long time, the process will be simple.

As with anything else, some people are resistant to long-term care insurance. I've met people who have a belief that long-term care insurance had some problems in the 1980s and 1990s. Back then, it's true that some insurance companies appeared to be fly-by-night institutions, which tainted the product for some people. Also, most of the insurance companies that offered long-term care insurance in the past didn't have the actuarial experience that they have now. So the biggest complaint that people had with long-term care insurance for many years was that it was overpriced. But in reality, the problem was that the insurance wasn't priced high enough. These companies hadn't anticipated that people would live for as long as they are living now. So because of the increase in life expectancy and also because of the rising cost of healthcare, insurance companies have had to increase their premiums in order to stay viable. Over the years, there has been some consolidation of businesses within the insurance industry. So now, if a company experiences problems, another insurance company will generally swoop in and buy it out.

Some people object to long-term care insurance by saying, "It's not going to happen to me." Or even, "If I get that sick, I won't need long-term care because I'll just kill myself."

To those objections, I simply say, "Yes, it may not happen to you, but it may." And, "No, you're not going to kill yourself."

Charging forward into your future without long-term care insurance is just like taking a gamble in life without medical insurance. There is a 40-50% chance that either you or your spouse will need long-term care. Those are some pretty high odds. Do you have homeowner's insurance on your home in case it burns down? What about automobile insurance for your car in case you get into an accident? The chances of your house going up in flames or of you ending up in a six-car pileup are slim compared to the 40% chance that either you or your spouse will enter a nursing facility for an extended stay in the future. Think about that. That's a pretty high percentage you're testing when you remain uninsured.

Everyone knows somebody whose sister or uncle or cousin was a vibrant, strong person who was into physical fitness until they found out that out of the blue, they acquired some sort of leukemia. You can never predict what might happen to your health.

No matter how good or secured you think your pension plan is, not having long-term care can actually threaten your financial stability in retirement. The only hole that most people have in their retirement planning is the huge expenditure that might incur because of long-term care. The purpose of designing a retirement plan is to ensure that you will have the quality of life that you've always dreamed of. But to be able to afford that ideal quality of life while juggling the additional long-term care expenditure of $50,000 to $100,000 a year would take most people down.

In other words, you're going to run out of money.

Many people tend to think in shorter time frames and fixate on the cost of putting money into a long-term care plan. But they don't consider the cost of potentially spending $80,000 to $100,000 more each year from their retirement plan. What if all of your money is in your IRA and you have to net out $100,000 for your medical expenses and also $50,000 for your spouse to live? Then you'd have to take out $150,000. But on top of that, you have to factor in the tax on that $150,000, which would be another $75,000 out of your pocket. That's $225,000 that you need to pull out every year. I hope you have a big pile of money! At that rate, even if you have two million dollars, you'll run dry in less than ten years. And what if you don't have two million dollars? What if you have only $800,000?

Long-term care insurance is about taking preventative measures so that you can protect your financial capital in your retirement. You're spending 1% now to protect the other 99% in the future. If you have a million dollar estate and you need to pay $10,000 each year to protect it from a possible spend-down of $300,000 to $500,000, I'd say that's a pretty good use of your money.

When you add on the life insurance company, the plan works even more in your favor. If you have a half a million-dollar life insurance component that has a $10,000 a month long-term care benefit and costs you $10,000, then you know that you'll recapture that $500,000 upon death. From a planning standpoint, this gives you the freedom to say to your spouse that they can go ahead and spend the IRA that's worth $500,000 or even spend it down on the care if you need to because you will replenish it with tax-free dollars.

Protect your pension from spend-down. And protect it from having to work twice as hard. If you have to pay money for your spouse from your pension and also pay money for your healthcare, then you're making your pension do double the amount of work it can handle. And if anything is forced to work twice as hard as anticipated, chances are that it will break down. Or stop altogether.

As you consider long-term care insurance, also think about your loved ones. Have a sober conversation with your spouse. Oftentimes, couples tell each other that if the other gets sick, then they'll do this and that and spend the rest of their lives caring for them. But what happens is that the caregiver ends up living a miserable life. If you get sick, is your spouse going to stay home and eat macaroni and cheese while sitting at your bedside? Or will she or he want to ride horses and take trips with the grandchildren? You don't want your spouse to forego the ideal quality of life because your healthcare is draining all your money.

People who care for chronically ill loved ones often become chronically ill themselves. A 75-year-old woman taking a 79-year-old man to the bathroom is okay for a little while, but those responsibilities will begin to take a toll on her as well, mentally, emotionally and physically. The caregiver often dies first. So if you have a spouse who is incapacitated, it's probably a better idea for both of you to have somebody else care for them than to have you take over those duties. This may sound a tad harsh, but it's a reality we all have to come to terms with. Long-term care enables you to maintain your quality of life and make sure that adequate care is given to the people that you love.

Then there are also the kids to think about. If your spouse is incapable of taking care of you and you have no long-term care plan in place, then your kids may have to step in and take care of you even as they manage their own careers and their own children. I have heard many people say that they spent years trying to convince their parents to get long-term care insurance, but that they didn't see the importance of it until it was too late. On the flip side, the children of people without long-term care plans tend to be the people who become converts to this type of planning because they've witnessed the need for long-term care coverage firsthand.

I recommend that you get long-term care now while you still can and while it's still affordable. Premiums go up almost exponentially as we get older. At a minimum, premiums for long-term care plans are between $3,000 and $10,000 depending on your current age. And costs are only rising.

If you're worried about how to fund your long-term care, there are ways to set up a side account with a guaranteed annuity to help you. You could set up a fund for $200,000 to kick off enough money to pay your benefit. And that $200,000 never has to be annuitized, so that benefit would go to the main beneficiaries. The income off of that account would go directly to fund the long-term care, so now you've protected $200,000 plus you've protected your entire pension from a possible spend-down of several hundred thousand dollars.

There is no such thing as a "one size fits all" pension plan. When you purchase your long-term care plan, go through an insurance agent who works with a bigger, well-known company. That agent can help you compare several different plans and customize one to fit your needs. They'll adjust your plan by taking into account factors such as the Cost of Living Adjustment, which would be better suited for someone who is 50 years old as opposed to someone who is 70 and will less likely benefit from it. Every plan that we recommend includes an in-home healthcare feature, which is the predominant choice for people who have money and want to receive treatment at home for as long as they can.

Your financial advisor can write your plan for you and as long as they're licensed and have the proper experience, they'll make sure that you don't overpay into your long-term care plan. I recommend that you go with someone who deals exclusively with retirees. Try to avoid someone who sells auto insurance, a little term-life insurance and says, "Oh by the way, our company offers a long-term care plan, too." You want to entrust your pension to someone who can answer all of your complicated questions and map out every possible scenario with you. I like to make sure that if I'm going to take the time to show somebody how to plan their pension, that we will do business together. If there is a reason that we wouldn't do business, such as a brother-in-law who is an insurance salesman, then I suggest that they consult that brother-in-law and then when they figure out what he does or doesn't know, they can come see me. We deal with retirees. All day and every day, it's all we do. And we specialize in protecting their wealth.

It's easy for a $700,000 estate or a million dollar estate to be spent down to nothing. When you have to take care of the deteriorating health of one or two people while paying an income, something's got to give.

Planning your pension is not complicated. All you have to do is determine how much money will be paid out on a daily basis, when the benefit will start and whether the money that you have is fixed or can be indexed for inflation. Then you factor in the possibility of getting sick. Nobody likes to think about getting sick, just as nobody likes to think about death. But these are decisions we all have to make. Even if you have the best personal pension plan in place, any serious medical ailment can derail those plans and all the work you spent to set up your retirement. You can make things significantly more complicated and deplete your personal pension later when you're also dealing with the stress of an illness, or you can keep things simple and protect that pension right now by hedging your health costs with long-term care insurance.

Chapter Seven

What About the Future?

We've talked about how to preserve financial security for retirement and how to insure your money against any catastrophic loss resulting from serious health conditions. Now that you and your spouse have a plan for creating the equivalent of your own pension, you're probably thinking about how to continue to provide for your children and grandchildren. In light of recent events, this is a very valid concern.

In the next 50 years, it will be harder to make and keep money in the United States due to our current economic conditions, exploding deficits, the inevitable increase in taxes, and etc. These conditions put more pressure on the financial system, so the probability for your wealth to be transferred across generations greatly diminishes with time. In this chapter, I will show you how you can preserve your financial legacy across generations through multi-generation skipping trusts, prevent unnecessary erosion of your assets, and establish further control over your wealth long after you pass away!

Oftentimes, your kids might have the necessary resources to provide for themselves, but they may need a little extra help with their own kids. With the rising costs of health care, private education, extracurricular activities, and both public and private college tuitions, this has become increasingly common. One method to set aside money directly for your grandchildren and protect it from estate taxes is to set up a multi-generational or generation-skipping trust. In this trust, you could put assets that could be appreciated, and shield them from any estate taxes.

There are limits to what you can place in a generation-skipping trust (GST), but there are no limits to what you can take out. The current limit imposed by the federal government is $1 million. One of the strategies for our clients is to reposition that one million dollar limit into premiums for a life insurance policy in a generation-skipping trust. If you put a million dollars in premiums, you can receive about five or six million dollars' worth of death benefit depending on the age of the insured. So, in essence, you can once again use life insurance to leverage your money five or six fold with this approach. And when you pass away, the grandkids now will receive that five or six million in that trust totally free of taxes. If it's set up properly, it will be completely protected from income taxes and estate taxes.

Again, we can use life insurance to recapture the wealth that might otherwise be lost and preserve it through the generations. Life insurance is probably the only financial product that provides the most amount of leverage on your money most efficiently. I could make one premium payment or one single deposit into a policy and it could pay a multiple of five, ten, or a thousand times more if I die the very next day. For example, let's say I bought a $3-million policy with a monthly premium payment of $5,000 a month. Now let's say that I make one payment, but then pass away the next day. The insurance company will then come in with $3 million after I only invest $5,000. What's the rate of return on that investment?

It's been shown time and time again that the most efficient manner to pass wealth down generations is through life insurance policies because of the potential rate of returns you can receive. You can get pennies on the dollar, and the benefit payment from life insurance policies often is tax-free. This is an outstanding feature because it allows you to prevent wealth erosion from estate taxes.

For example, when Bob Brooks, the founder of the Hooters restaurant chain died, the value of the Hooters chain was around $250 million. But when he left the chain to his estate, there were estate tax obligations that had to be met. Because Bob Brooks didn't have the proper estate planning in place, the family had to sell the business in order to meet the estate tax obligations. Had Bob Brooks repositioned some of his wealth into a proper life insurance policy, the taxes on the estate, which may have been around $100 million, could be paid by that life insurance policy and the family could have retained ownership of the company. They might have spent $20 million or $25 million on that policy, but that would still be cheaper than paying the full $100 million and selling the business. In the end, the Brooks family was forced to sell the business in a fire sale because buyers knew they need money, so the Brooks family didn't get top dollar on the sale, and they still had to pay the full tax bill. Consequently, the value of the Brooks estate after all these transactions was far less than what it should have been with the proper estate planning.

So I always tell my clients that if they are serious about preserving their wealth and passing it on to their heirs, they need to reposition their assets into life insurance policies. If you think about it, if you have $4 million, and there's $300,000 that is set aside in a reserve fund that you will never ever touch because it would be your last $300,000. Why not take that and put it inside a life insurance policy that is going to guarantee a million dollar payoff? It just makes sense. You could still access it if you need to under certain conditions, but chances are, you would never ever touch it because you would have to spend the other $3.7 million down to zero. And that's not going to happen. So I'll advise my clients to take that $300,000 and leverage it to create a positive arbitrage through life insurance.

Now say you reposition an amount of $500,000. Depending on the percentage of how much life insurance you can buy, with this single premium payment, you could take the overall estate from $4 million to $6 million. When we do this, we'll want to make sure that the additional money we create through the policy is set up in an irrevocable insurance trust that will not be added to our estate value for estate tax purposes. Now we've just increased the value of our estate by $2 million tax-free.

And that's the true value of estate planning!

Additionally, the income that could be generated from $5 or $6 million obviously would be taxable depending on how it was invested later. The $6 million could potentially create an income stream of $250,000 to $280,000 a year for the children, or in this case, the grandchildren. If that money is not needed, it can simply accrue. So now, the grandchildren have a built-in retirement plan as well. Then, what they should do immediately upon having children themselves, or upon their children having children, is set up a generation-skipping trust for their children's children to keep the flow going. So the money from one generation can benefit multiple generations. This is an excellent planning approach that is often overlooked.

Now even though you can take care of future generations through proper estate planning, there still are no guarantees that our children or their children will be good financial stewards. Many clients worry about what happens if the kids spend all the money. This is also a valid concern and in proper estate planning you can retain control of your assets long after you've passed.

All you need to do to retain control is to set up the trust properly. We often say in our office that a trust allows you to maintain control from beyond the grave. Essentially, you can put in place any stipulations as you desire. And there are many strategies and guidelines you can have in place to achieve your wishes in how the money is distributed, to whom, and by whom, whether it be a trustee or your most responsible heir. In addition, you can make all of your stipulations and guidelines be revocable should certain events transpire that might lead you to change your mind if you were otherwise alive. So essentially, nothing has to be set in stone when you die unless you desire it. Proper estate planning should evolve and continue to live out your wishes, even if you do not!

In our office, we've seen many clients come in and worry about their children squandering their entire estate. When we work with them on planning their estate, we've used many strategies in alleviating this concern. One such strategy might be layering the amount they might receive in the trust. For example, if I die and I'm sixty years old and my daughter is thirty, she might not get all the money at age thirty. I could layer it where she receives 10% at age 30, another 10% at age 40, and then at age 50, she might get 25%, and so on.

Another strategy might be to set up a stream of income within the trust and say that your children can only live off the interest on the trust. The only circumstances where they will be allowed to erode the principle inside the trust are for medical necessity.

We've also had instances where clients say under no circumstances are you going to give Billy anything more than $100,000 a year. So, if his leg has fallen off, Billy doesn't get more than $100,000 per year. Usually, these are instances where Billy might take that money and do something that might endanger himself even more. These instances might be due to substance abuse, mental illness, special needs, and etc. There are a number of areas where the heirs may not be able to handle those assets themselves, and may need a little guidance with it.

There are even stipulations you can place inside the trust to serve as motivational tools. Years ago, I worked with some guys who were "trust fund babies," and some of the those trust funds had guidelines that stated if they made $100,000 a year on their own, the trust would then pay an additional $100,000 to match. So it created an incentivized environment where it motivated them to work as hard as possible to earn their own keep. Because whatever they were able to bring to the table, the trust would then match it!

Other stipulations you can create inside the trust may dictate where the assets are distributed. Often times, we have met with clients that have said, "I have one child that's very responsible, and I have one that is not very good with money." So we might distribute a million or two to the fiscally responsible child because they won't blow it. But the other one might take the money to Vegas and never be heard from again, so we may want to put in more stringent guidelines for the other.

Other times, we may have a child that has special needs, so we might set up the trust to distribute more to that child. In these instances, the other children are usually more sympathetic as well. This may be due to more selfish reasons — they might want enough set aside in a trust so they don't have to take over care of that sibling when the parents are no longer around.

Sometimes, although less frequent, we'll also have instances where clients have written off the children totally from their inheritance. These are instances where the client might have five children, but only three are getting the inheritance because the other two are estranged beyond repair. Other times, it is due to divorce, and the two kids might live and side with their mother. So the client will only leave an inheritance for his three kids because the other two may be taken care of by the mother, who might leave out his three.

There are also times where our clients have felt the need to distribute their wealth outside of their immediate heirs. This might be due to a variety of reasons, but the best way to make sure your money goes to where you want it to go is through a trust that you create. A number of clients say, "I'm going to give my kids about a million dollars each, but the rest of the money is going to charity because I don't think the kids need more than a million." So they'll leave it to a foundation, a non-profit, or their church or synagogue.

Despite all these benefits and options in estate planning and trusts, we still see many people who have hesitations and resistance to the idea of proper estate planning. Often, these people are the perfect candidates for estate planning. For example, they might have a net worth of $4 million, but they are using $2.5 million of that $4 million to generate their retirement income. The other $1.5 million may be in other assets such as real estate. So they'll say, "Well, you know, the kids will get the house," and so they'll keep the house until they pass. Again, our main concern with that plan is the risks involved. In a few years, who knows what the house will be worth? In the old days, we could say a $1.5 million house will be worth $3 or $4 million when you die. These days, we'll be lucky if it's still worth $1.5 million. But if some of that were positioned into life insurance, we would have leverage. Say we had $500,000 properly positioned and we could get a $2 million policy with it. So now, you've got $2 million instead of $500,000.

We also see hesitation over the perceived control or perceived loss of control of assets. No one wants to sell a house, or maybe the beach house. It might be for sentimental reasons. Our clients will think, "We'll just give the beach house to the kids and they'll be fine." But what if you give the kids $2 million, and they could buy their own beach house and still have a $1.5 million left over in tax-free money? Wouldn't that be a much better deal?

Other times, we see people who do not think about estate planning because they think their children are doing better than they are. But we often say that the future is completely unpredictable and things can happen overnight. Businesses can go out of business, even very large companies. A few years ago, no one would have thought that Lehman Brothers would go out of business. No one imagined that GM or Ford would have the problems that they had. Even more, the children that are in great financial shape today may have disabilities in the future. They might go through divorce, or have economic conditions unrelated to their ability to produce just thrust upon them. So somebody that's in great financial shape today might be wiped out 10 or 15 years. Proper estate planning could alleviate the risks in the future.

Even more, the importance of leveraging your estate is so critical because a million dollars in the future might not do a lot. It could be the equivalent of $400,000 or $500,000. That's quite a discount. So without the proper estate planning with leveraging through life insurance, we might not see our savings or our estate go as far as we would like.

But with proper planning and the use of life insurance policies as leverage, you could produce tangible rates of return that would extend your estate generations into the future. If you look at some of the internal rates of return from life insurance policies, you'll find that it is 5% or 6% net of taxes, or 7% or 8% guaranteed for 25 years. What other investment can you buy that's going to guarantee you anywhere from 4% to 6% guaranteed net of taxes? I can't think of any. And these rates of return are if we span twenty-five to thirty years. What if the event happens in fifteen years? The rate of return is more like 12% to 15%, guaranteed, net of taxes. I think that's phenomenal!

I can't think of any reason why anyone wouldn't want to properly plan their estate and dictate how their assets are distributed. It is just as important as putting a will in place because you can: put on all kinds of stipulations, require that certain goals be met before your children get money, dictate who handles and serves as the trustee of your assets, and more! You can be as creative as you want to be. But the bottom line is, if you don't properly plan out your state, it's going to be the government who gets your assets.

This is always a discussion that we always have with our clients in our office because control of assets is as important as the assets themselves. And when it comes to planning our clients' retirement or after-retirement, we always make sure that their assets are structured in such a fashion guarantees them a stream of income for multiple generations, without being subject to the risks that life may present. We believe that's the most efficient use of capital, and it will make life a whole lot easier for you and your loved ones for generations to come.

Chapter Eight

Should We Talk?

Let's review briefly what we've discussed. In this book, we explored how you can give yourself a pension even though traditional pension plans through employers no longer exist. We saw how the equity markets can never provide the stable returns we require for security in retirement, given the inherent risks of uncertainty. As a result, we saw how we can utilize new financial products like fixed indexed deferred annuities to create a personal pension from a guaranteed stream of income, all while maintaining full control of your savings principal. You now are able to receive the same financial freedom similar to the pension your grandfather received when he received the gold watch on retirement.

We also learned how we can protect against uncertainties in life, such as accidents and death, to preserve our retirement security if we need to rely on our spouses' pension or social security. You should now have the peace of mind of knowing that you are not going to run out of money. In addition, we saw how we can leverage life insurance and long-term care insurance intelligently to mitigate any risk from disability and death. Utilizing these strategies, you can take care of your spouse, your children and your grandchildren now and after you pass away! Furthermore, we saw how we can exponentially increase the value of our estate by leveraging life insurance policies in generation-skipping trusts, and leave an indelible financial legacy for generations!

The next step is to take action! Life always has a great deal of uncertainty to it and you never want to be caught without the financial protection you need to have a secure retirement and take care of your loved ones! After you put down this book, make the call and find the appropriate professionals in your area that specializes in retirement and estate planning. Or simply call the professional who gave you this book.

You want to meet with a financial planner with an expertise in passing wealth on to the next generation or two. They should have extensive experience in retirement and estate planning. And if they have done it before, they should be able to show you the kinds of strategies they employed with their other clients and the positive results they achieved. After that, it's just a measure of determining how much would be appropriate to put into something like a generation-skipping trust or a large life insurance policy.

You are welcome to contact us through our website and we can direct you to somebody that does this type of planning in your area. As the saying goes, a year too soon is better than a day too late.

In our office, we typically serve individuals at or near retirement with a minimum of $250,000 or more in investable assets. If these characteristics describe you, and if you are interested in custom-tailored strategies you can employ to guarantee your retirement and increase your assets, we invite you to give us a call at our office *today*! We can create a plan in detail to maximize your savings and preserve your assets into perpetuity.

Here's how our process works. We will make an assessment of your financial situation. Then we'll show you how you can structure your retirement savings more efficiently and protect those savings for the long term. Usually, we can get you on a solid retirement plan within one to three months after doing the assessment. After the plan is implemented, we will monitor your account on an annual basis to ensure that your information on the account is accurate and the plan is on track.

I want to really stress the importance of meeting with a professional here. Everyone's financial situation is different and there should be customized strategies employed to meet your personal retirement goals. For example, in the past, I've sometimes advised clients to spend down their IRA accounts, and other times, I have told them not to touch the IRA account, but spend the other money they have saved first in order to let the IRA grow a little more before we need to be taxed on it.

The point is that everyone's situation is going to be different. That's why it is so important to work with a professional that deals specifically with retirees. The strategies we employ for someone who made $50,000 a year his entire life are different than someone who has made $500,000 a year simply due to the taxes they may face. The introductory knowledge you learned from this book should only provide basic background into the potential strategies that are available for securing your retirement. Always meet with a professional to when developing your own personal retirement plans. The benefits you receive from proper retirement and estate planning will always exceed the minimal fees involved.

So please don't hesitate! You never know what might happen tomorrow and when it comes to securing your future and taking care of your loved ones, you always want to be prepared. You want to have a solid plan for your financial matters in place because that is how you will truly feel liberated. Once we help you get that plan in place and you see how you now have a guaranteed stream of income for the rest of your life, all while leaving a healthy inheritance to your loved ones, you will fully be able to enjoy the fruits of your lifetime of labor. With solid plans in place, you can enjoy the retirement…and the peace of mind…that you and your loved ones deserve.

About the Author

Michael Steranka, CEO of Retirement Planning Services, Inc. has been helping people plan for their retirement for over twenty years. Focusing on all insurance aspects for the client, Mike has a passion for protecting retirees' assets and helping them safely reach their retirement income planning goals.

As a professional concerned with the health, financial and social issues facing retirees Mike has received comprehensive education and training throughout his career including being an Ed Slott Master Elite Advisor.

Michael recently co-authored *The E Myth Financial Advisor (Why Most Financial Advisory Firms Don't Work and What To Do About It)* with world renowned small business guru Michael E. Gerber. *The E Myth Financial Advisor* outlines the systems and procedures that financial people need to add to their practices in order to ensure success.

Ed Slott, CPA and Founder of IRAhelp.com said this about *The E Myth Financial Advisor,* "Michael Steranka has outlined how to systematize your planning practice. **This is a must-read for all advisors looking to grow their practice!**"

In *Retire Now,* Michael reduces many of the complex decisions retirees need to make in order to achieve successful retirement. In a series of easy to follow steps, Mike takes the reader on their own personal journey so they can empower themselves to make the right choices for themselves and their families.

Special Note from Mike Steranka

In this hectic world we live in it is nice to know that simple solutions for retirement are readily available. You have an opportunity to meet with professionals like the one featured on this book to see how they can frame your retirement income. This book was written specifically for pre-retirees and those already retired.

The systems, procedures and proprietary income planning software we have used to effectively retire over 1,000 couples in the Washington, D.C. Metro area are being shared with advisors from coast to coast. Chances are you were given this book by a professional whom I have personally consulted with.

Make sure you contact that individual to say thanks for the book and please visit them so they can show you the types of planning outlined in this book. It will be well worth your time.

Notes

Notes

CPSIA information can be obtained
at www.ICGtesting.com
Printed in the USA
BVOW08s0019180917
495093BV00010B/159/P